C000193862

LOFTS

OF AMSTERDAM

LOFTS
OF AMSTERDAM

Printed by Snoeck-Ducaju & Zoon, Ghent

©   2000   TECTUM PUBLISHERS
                 Hessenstraatje, 3
                 2000 Antwerp, Belgium

ISBN   90 | 76886 | 03 | 2
WD   2000 | 9021 | 3

(2)

FOREWORD

Lofts of Amsterdam is a marvellous book illustrating in word and image the possibility of reusing as homes warehouses and other buildings not intended for habitation. Whereas in many other European cities warehouses and other industrial buildings have for a long time remained empty after their original function was discontinued, in Amsterdam they have been used creatively as places in which to live and work, partly as a result of the great shortage of housing several decades ago. But it was not only at the lower end of the housing market that these unusual living spaces proved attractive. Their unpredictable interior subdivisions and dimensions meant they provided solutions for a whole range of prospective occupiers.

The reuse of these buildings displays respect for the history and for the scale and rhythm of the city. It is in accordance with the policies of the city's and the country's administration, which is oriented towards sustainability. That which is of value and use must be preserved. One cannot treat the past carefully enough.

What is so pleasing in this book is that it offers a broad view of the many possibilities, in the various price ranges, of refurbishing a warehouse.

Loft-like dwellings have come into being in expensive and less expensive buildings at several places in old Amsterdam. The text and the pictures of interiors show an infectious multiformity of lifestyles. These lofts thereby make an entirely individual contribution to a multiform city.

MR S. PATIJN
Mayor

CONTENTS

FOREWORD   5

INTRODUCTION   9

THE HISTORY OF THE AMSTERDAM'S WAREHOUSES   11

LVIVNG AND WORKING   17

OPEN LOFTS   49

COMMERCIAL PROMISES   85

COLLECTORS   103

CHURCHES   139

H₂O   165

FROM JUGENDSTIL TO MINIMALISM   181

IN THE BEGINNING   233

ACKNOWLEDGEMENTS   245

Tectum Publishers are especially grateful to Inge Vyt, managing director of Isis Beheer B.V. Tilburg project development and financing, whose contribution helped make it possible to publish this book.

INTRODUCTION

Lofts of Amsterdam is a richly illustrated book providing a survey of fifty marvellous lofts in the Dutch capital. More and more people are looking for a personal way of living, for a place that fully fits their lifestyle, a location where they feel completely at home. A loft is a good example of a highly individual form of living.

The original English meaning of the word – a storeroom under the roof – no longer sufficiently covers its use. Loft-dwellers find their perfect homes not only in former warehouses but just as well in schools, churches, hospitals, stations and canteens. They often have hidden qualities. The most distinctive elements emerge when the soul of the building is revealed.

The wealth of a loft is often found in its decor and atmosphere.

Designing a loft is a challenge. Large areas, concrete columns, rough materials and thick walls demand an inventive approach. Lofts are in demand not only as homes – companies also like them for their offices or showrooms. In the Netherlands, Amsterdam steals the show when it comes to the number of lofts. After all, nowhere else will you find between 600 and 700 surviving warehouses.

Lofts of Amsterdam is a book in which you will discover the charm of a view of living in which freedom and non-conformity dominate.

THE HISTORY OF AMSTERDAM'S WAREHOUSES

Since so many of the stones of Amsterdam are overloaded with history, it is a delight to cast our minds back to the past. In addition, warehouses have defined the face of the city for centuries. There is no other city in Europe with such a large number of industrial monuments. The reason for this is that in the seventeenth century Amsterdam was the world's staple: almost all the goods traded throughout the world were stored in Amsterdam warehouses.

The old thirteenth-century core was formed by the buildings round Dam, Damrak, Warmoesstraat and Nieuwendijk. Warmoesstraat was the most important, where many wealthy merchants lived in stone houses. Their warehouses lay at the waterside behind the houses, so that the ships in the Damrak could easily unload. The fact that rich people lived in these merchants' houses with their warehouses attached, is expressed in the average rentable value of the houses in the Warmoesstraat.

On the east side it was 74 pounds, and on the west, the water-side, 133 pounds. At the Damrak the average rent was 102 pounds. These were the 'most expensive' streets in Amsterdam in the fourteenth, fifteenth and sixteenth centuries. Most of the residents here were traders and merchants. Until about 1600 the goods were kept in the storage lofts at the top of the merchants' houses. As trade grew, the need for storage space increased.

At the start of the sixteenth century, warehouses and merchants' homes were build in great numbers along the broad defensive canals. They opened onto the quayside along the canals and not onto a street, as the older houses in Warmoesstraat and Nieuwendijk had. In this new scheme of things the canal acted as an inland port and the street in front of the merchants' houses and warehouses as a quay on

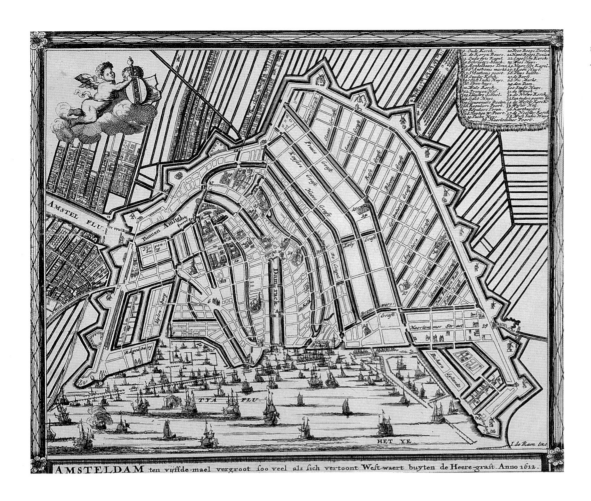

'Amsteldam ten vijfde mael vergroot soo veel als sich vertoont westwaerts buyten de Heeregraft'
Amsterdam 1612, engraving 160 × 180 mm.

Nieuwe Teertuinen 19 to 15 (r. to l.) Looking towards bridge no. 321 ('Sloterdijkerbrug') and the start of Sloterdijkstraat. Left is the 'de Roosos' tar company with a hoist to lift the barrels of tar out of the barges on the canal (the last windlass in Amsterdam). Photo Olie Jansz. Jacob (1834-1905)

1st November 1896. 'Nieuwe vaart. Panorama looking north-west from the De Gooyer corn mill, Funenkade 5. Foreground: Dageraadsbrug (bridge no. 353) in front of Sarphatistraat. Left: land at the rear of the Hoogte Kadijk. Right: Oostenburgergracht - Witteburgergracht - Kattenburgergracht (r. to l.). Photo Olie Jansz. Jacob (1834-1905)

which the goods could be unloaded and stored, to be easily transported on by ship or wagon. This is in contrast to the old warehouses on the Damrak where there was no quay, and which had become poorly accessible to horse and cart as a result of the increasing density of building. Amsterdam played an important transit role, with many goods being transported on after a short or long term of storage. The more efficiently this took place the less it cost. That the new arrangement worked well at the two moat quaysides was apparent from the fact that in the second half of the sixteenth century a continuous quay was also constructed along the west side of the Damrak. After this the warehouses were much more accessible, and this area developed into the most important trading centre in the Nieuwe Zijde. The shifting of the front façades of the houses to the side nearest the quay was a confirmation of the new situation.

The distinction between living and working did not exist in the sixteenth and seventeenth centuries, when in most cases they were integrated or ran side by side. Just as in the Middle Ages the merchant did his office work in his front building, lived behind and above, and had his storage space in the loft, in the late sixteenth century too there were numerous merchants who used part of their house for business purposes. This is because, however much the late sixteenth-century residents of the canal houses wished to live 'in a good area', they never lost their commercial attitude. The storage of goods remained an important matter. The considerable length of the quay had to be made useful. After all, the cost of its construction, paid for by those who lived there, had to be recovered.

Like merchants' houses, the warehouses are narrow, deep and high. Their average depth is easily thirty metres, which was also the depth of most of the merchants' houses along the main canals. But there is one difference: the merchants' houses consist of a front and a rear building separated by a courtyard, whereas warehouses comprised a single building extending over the entire depth. Warehouses are easily recognised by their vertical row of loft windows with shutters. These windows often had a round arch, but there are also warehouses with rectangular windows. Most warehouses have a fluted gable, and these were still being built well into the eighteenth century. There is little difference between the seventeenth and eighteenth-century warehouses. The Amsterdam warehouse was

being built for centuries with few changes. This often makes them hard to date. All the warehouses in Amsterdam have hoist-beams, often with splendid hoisting equipment. It was soon discovered that these hoist-beams were useful for getting household goods inside too.

There are several types of warehouse: single, double, consisting of two identical buildings, terraced warehouses, rhythmical rows of alternating wide and narrow warehouses, grain and arms warehouses and storehouses. The most common is the ordinary single warehouse with the same width as a normal merchant's house, which is five to eight metres. We often find them in rows, as terraced warehouses. In Amsterdam, one also finds double warehouses with a width of fifteen metres. This type often has two identical fluted gables, but they also exist with a single trapezium-shaped gable. The large warehouse complexes, or storehouses, were owned by the city or such huge companies as the VOC [East-India Company]. The biggest warehouse was the Oost-Indisch Zeemagazijn [East-India Maritime Storehouse] built in 1661. This huge building was two hundred and fifteen metres wide. It collapsed in 1822 as a result of poor maintenance.

The nineteenth and twentieth-century ware-

Top left: *1891. Brouwersgracht, nos. 68, 70, 72*
Top right: *c. 1890. Nieuwe Vaart, nos. 5-11*
Bottom left: *c. 1890. Barges being loaded and unloaded*
Bottom right: *c. 1950. Entrepôt-dok, nos. 12, 12a, 13, etc.*
  Gemeentelijke Handelsinrichtingen

houses built on the shores of the IJ are a different story. They were often called *'vemen'* [storage companies] after the businesses that ran them. Silos were also built. A remarkably large number of warehouses have been preserved in Amsterdam, somewhere between six and seven hundred. Along some canals almost all the buildings are warehouses, as on Brouwersgracht and Oude Schans. Prinseneiland consists almost entirely of warehouses. There are also a great many along Prinsengracht and Oudezijds Kolk.

Plenty of Amsterdam warehouses have now been converted into lofts. To make this possible

Top left: *7.3.1890. Prinseneiland, nos. 100-119, looking towards 't Achterom*
Top right: *1902. Entrepôt-dok, nos. 29-34*
Bottom left: *c.1950. Entrepôt-dok, no. 85*
Bottom right: *18.4.1968. Plantage Muidergracht, no. 65*

the shutters have been replaced by glazed windows, though in a few cases the open shutters have been retained. This means their appearance has radically changed: in the past the shutters usually remained shut.

Just as in London and New York, it was in the first place artists who saw the potential of these empty warehouses as places in which to live and work. Legal or otherwise, draughts or no draughts, there was space and light and they were affordable. Until the city council also realised that these neglected buildings had a future. Project developers jumped on the band-

wagon and before long even adventurous flat-dwellers were queueing up to live in one of these lofts too.

LIVING...

AND WORKING

*Why look for a separate building or studio
if you have enough space in your own loft?
There is no need for your private life and your work
to get in each other's way,
since a loft usually provides sufficient space for expansion.
Artists and independent entrepreneurs in particular
prefer this type of home.*

Everything has been chosen and designed with care.

The owner's work is everywhere: lying, standing or hanging.
It is no coincidence that this home is often used as a gallery.

A studio space can be made by pulling out the sliding panels.

THE ART OF OMISSION

The designer and artist André Martens has created his ideal home
in part of a former Jewish monastery. The basis is an all-inclusive design,
every part of which forms a unity. Sliding panels offer the possibility of
creating several spaces, the furniture is mobile, and storage space is as far as
possible incorporated into the walls. The materials make for a bright
organic atmosphere.

The materials used in the bathroom give it the air of a temple.

So as to make best use of every square metre the kitchen is tucked away under the void.

An extra room is concealed behind a fully-revolving wall.

An impressive loft with a sturdy beam structure and industrial windows.

CRACK THE SAFE

A loft with humour and a glint in its eye. The present occupier of this former bank building has kept the original heavy safe door with its combination lock as the entrance to the kitchen. The design of the bathroom is hugely original: the floor is covered with pebbles, the white and coloured wash goes into separate wash-baskets through two round holes in the wall, and drinks can be handed through a hatch from the kitchen. Another amazing invention is the fully revolving wall, four metres by six, behind which is an extra room.

The original door of the safe was incorporated into the loft in an extraordinary way.

Beyond the safe door is the kitchen.

And the bathroom floor? A pebble beach!

The solid, sturdy beams of this former merchant's house give the loft great charm.

ART AT HOME

This distinctive building on an Amsterdam canal is a home to artists.
The loft, with its dozens of objects from all over the world, breathes
a special atmosphere and warmth. All this is enhanced even more by
original heavy beams. A short tour: a French *fleurs plantes herbes* oak kitchen
cupboard, American office chairs from Boston, a display case for a collection
of miniature shoes, an 1880 chair from the concert hall in Liège, Chinese
drawings on silk, a Provençal dining table, and much, much more.

Roof-lights at the back provide sufficient light.

*The whole loft acts as a setting for the inhabitants' own work,
and also for that of other artists.*

The mezzanine can be reached by indoor stairs in wood and metal.

A long Provençal dining table and an industrial kitchen by Cooking Factory combine harmoniously.

A collection of little shoes is displayed in a glass case.

Artists' work is regularly exhibited.

The bathroom adjoins the bedroom.

Big old cabinets, a wooden floor and a visible wooden roof structure give this loft a hint of the countryside. This pleasant atmosphere is accentuated by the personal collection of old furniture, sculpture, books and other objects.

RURAL SCENES

On the Western islands, and especially on Bickerseiland and Prinseneiland, a fair number of artists have settled in the plentiful warehouses. One of them, Peter van der Heijden, lives and works on the top two floors of an old warehouse.

Jens Pfeifer's deer gracefully bows its head in the serene corner where music is frequently listened to.

LIFE IS A PROCESS OF GROWTH

The artist Iris Eichenberg lives and works in a former contractor's workhouse. Her studio is at the front and her spacious living area at the back. But dwelling and workplace merge together. If something is in the right-hand corner one day, it may be on the left the next. Household implements may end up in the studio, and works of art are to be viewed in the kitchen cupboard.

Life is a process of growth, and her loft clearly reflects this.

A faded kilim, knitted red hearts on the floor and a portrait by Marlène Dumas.
This plain, intriguing space is art.

Light, as in a gallery, emptiness, as in a studio.

The artist has given the narrow dark-grey table a woollen coat.

The kitchen cupboard is filled not only with provisions,
but also miscellaneous curios and parts which the occupant
reuses in her own work.

The kitchen cum living room radiates a pleasant atmosphere through the iron windows with their old-fashioned catches, the varied collection of chairs and the big dresser.

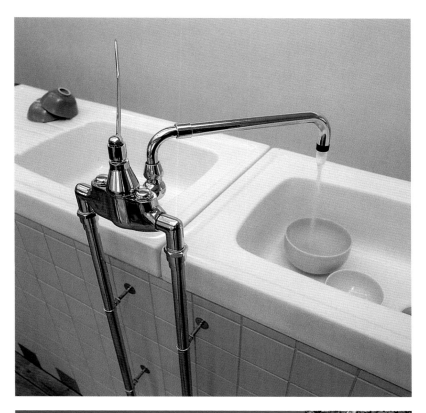

The laboratory tap over the French porcelain sink is mounted separately.

The patio is in the middle of the original canteen.
The window frames are painted the petrol blue characteristic of the old bridges of Paris.

SELF DEVISED AND HOMEMADE

This former company canteen was hidden away on the inner area behind a row of houses. Its new owners immediately saw its potential, despite its poor condition and the mass of work needed to make it habitable once more. They devised and made everything themselves, from kitchen to patio, from works of art to furniture.

Opposite the sitting area is the work-space, with desk and drawing board. The cherrywood filing cabinet was made by the owners, and the bluestone top was found amongst demolition material.

The bath on its legs gives a nostalgic feeling to the otherwise soberly finished space with its austere washing corner and shower room.

The sitting area is under one of the large skylights. The sofa by Eileen Gray was the only 'real' purchase. The rest of the furniture they made themselves or picked up for nothing and later restored. The two Art Deco chairs, for example, are in the style of the Berlage school. The floor, which covers the entire loft, is in rough scrap wood and is deliberately left this way.

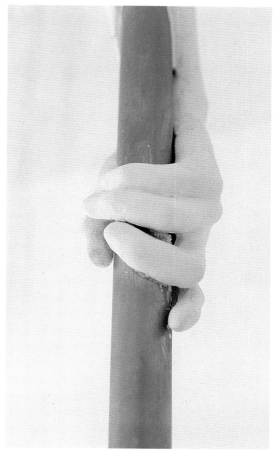

The plaster hands were cast from his and hers.

FROM PICASSO TO WOLKERS

This building in an old Jewish neighbourhood first housed a diamond cutters and later a technical school.

Without radically modifying the structure, the owners have still adapted it to their own needs, flexibility being the key word. Work, domestic life and relaxation mingle and are not tied to particular rooms. With its mobile table and wheeled shop counter, the decor can be altered in an instant.
The eye-catchers include a four-metre wide mirror, a fire to a design by Picasso, an old pianola, a work of art by Jan Wolkers and a rope to climb or sit on.

An amusing detail is the pair of plaster hands tightly gripping the railing on the mezzanine balcony.

The owner created an additional floor with a balcony
to make better use of the seven metres height.

An old shop counter with drawers was bought from a Belgian antique dealer.

Wheels under the bed enable it to be moved to another space quite simply.

A gigantic dried water-lily adorns the wall.

The bathroom is restrained,
with freestanding basins.

OPEN LOFTS

The openness of a loft is usually
one of its greatest charms.
By respecting the original structure
and not subdividing the interior too much,
the occupiers retain the freedom to grow in parallel with their home.
It is precisely its open spaces
that made it easy to change a loft's decor.

The original form of the windows, the wooden shutters, the rough brick and the flagstones on the ground floor are reminiscent of a farm.

The colourful geometric painting breaks the industrial impression made by the red-painted concrete floor.
This huge space seems endless, partly as a result of the moveable furniture
that can be rolled wherever desired.

FROM STABLE TO MEGA-LOFT

These former stables from 1850, with a total area of five hundred twenty square metres, are now used as a living space for the whole family. Downstairs, it feels just like a farm, warm and cosy.

Upstairs, the continuous high ceilings with their wooden beams and the large windows make a fine contrast with the separate corners for the work room, the bedrooms and the bathroom.

Everything here revolves around light, restfulness and order.

Galvanised shelving against the wall provides plenty of archive space.

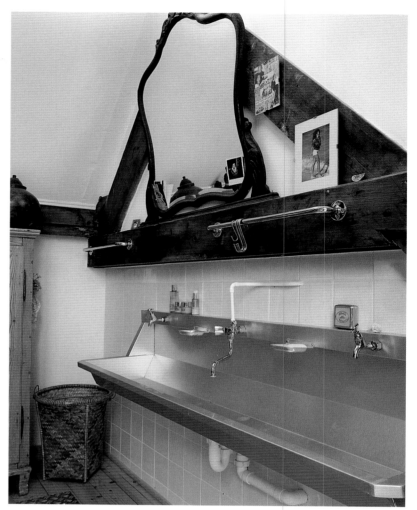

Sit on a wooden garden bench while waiting for the bath. The long wash basin has space for all the family.

Everyone has their own 'corner' in the hundred square metre communal bedroom.

Everything here has to do with form and function. The kitchen floor for example is a easy and hygienic steel sheet, and the waste-pipe floats in the air, so that the kitchen was able to be installed straight onto the concrete floor.

The right-angles of the cube can be clearly seen in the kitchen too.
The heavy iron front door provides security.

LIVING IN BOXES

A large open space with two closed 'boxes'. It's clear that the people who live here have a boundless sense of loft design. After their first child was born, bedroom-cubes seemed to be the ideal solution for the privacy needed. This use of boxes creates a distinct division of the remaining space. The obliquely positioned cubes also act as playful partitions. Combined with the use of such materials as steel, wood and plastic, the floor plan gives a good idea of what one can achieve in a loft.

The open bathroom on its platform is behind the bedroom.
This means the owners can withdraw and enjoy a bath.

The occupants sleep in cube-like rooms of their own design.
The parents and children have their own houses
within the spacewhole.

On the bedroom wall hangs a highly individual text in ice-blue neon.
The shoes hanging on tightly stretched cables in front of the window present a comical sight.

ELECTRIC BLUE

The artist Marijke de Goey transformed this four hundred and eighty square metre space in an old dressmaker's workshop into a place in which to live and work. The high, open space is filled with works of art, countless objects and moveable furniture. The cool shades of blue and the use of iron, concrete and glass even makes it look a little futuristic. The only place the artist can withdraw to is the very original bedroom, an intimate enclosed space floating above the kitchen.

An iron construction runs like a thread throughout the loft.

Everything has a function, all manner of collections have been given a home, even in the hollows of the beams, such as these model cars and shoes.

The loft's height enables one to enjoy the whole space from the industrial catwalk specially made for this purpose.

The rhythm of the roof is repeated in round paper lamps.

A long table of broken glass was designed by the owner herself.
The deliberate omission of bannisters from the stairs that twist their way
upwards emphasises their flowing lines.

Few are favoured with a glimpse of the artist Marijke de Goey, here at
work at her drawing board and work-tables.

The same space, but now more than fifty years ago and not quite so unusual…

A view of the loft before conversion.

MATERIALS SPEAK FOR THEMSELVES

Austere but atmospheric: that is the best way to describe this former brewery warehouse. This gigantic place, handed over in its original state, had to be substantially converted. Both the occupiers and the architect Casper Schuuring advocate allowing the authentic colours and materials to express themselves, in this case wood, concrete and terrazzo. The three hundred square metre space was left largely open. Striking elements include the great steel doors with their exceptional hinges. Under-floor heating and two electric heaters keep the space warm. This loft is a quiet oasis close to the busy Albert Cuypmarkt.

The concrete columns, the white walls and the almost empty space all add to the feel of an authentic loft.

In the kitchen a terrazzo concrete block was chosen as a worktop.

The austere Spartan style is extended into the bathroom.

The inhabitants also opted for terrazzo concrete for the bath.

Full-width concrete steps lead to the bedroom.

Considerable renovation work was needed to clean the place up.

The entrance to the loft is through a big solid-iron door.

In the centre of the sitting and reading corner are two bent cane chairs.

The minimal amount of furniture leaves plenty of free space.

VIEW OF THE CITY

On the top floor of a monumental building at the heart of Amsterdam city centre, is this cosy penthouse whose hospitality, snugness and originality strike one immediately.
The use of partitions and cubes is ingenious. The sense of space and the number of rooms comes as a surprise, while the view from the roof terrace, which covers no less than two hundred seventy square metres, is simply breathtaking.

ll the classic ingredients of a loft are found here: pillars, a wooden floor and a beamed ceiling.

A library, kitchen and scullery are located behind a grey glass wall.

The kitchen, in blue-grey and stainless steel, is large enough for full-scale culinary exploits.

The worktop is lit by reading lamps.

Every room, whether it be bathroom, bedroom or kitchen, has been created by means of partitions and cubes.

A glass top panel between wall and ceiling ensures unity throughout the loft and light in every room.

Rectangular tiles reminiscent of the underground railway follow the line of the bathroom. The basin is set onto the raised bath surround whereby it all forms a single piece.

In the middle of the space a staircase leads to the glass superstructure where one encounters heaven on earth:
a marvellous roof terrace with a fantastic view.

A space like this demands emptiness, so that each furnished corner spontaneously assumes its own identity.

Endless! That describes the breathtaking staircase that rises from the hall to the guest rooms and roof terrace.

SCHOOL OF ORIGINAL DESIGN

It is in the exact spot where two classrooms and a corridor of a former school building stood that one now finds this predominantly white loft. The smells and colours of the school have faded now, to be replaced by light, air and space. Functional classroom furniture has made way for strikingly original designs. Dashing children and school bells are a thing of the past, now people live and work here in peace and quiet.

The metallic blue of the fine supporting pillar stands out well.

Next to the big door in the hall you come across the feather-light knotted chair by the designer Marcel Wanders.

In the room with the fireplace hangs Rody Graumans' '85-bulb lamp' from the Droog Design collection.
The white and orange chairs are by Rietveld.

Behind the sitting area there is an extra living room mainly for winter use.
Galvanised bookcases rise to the very top of the turret room, thereby forming a real library.

The kitchen is cleverly tucked away in a grey cube.
Big round holes in the ceiling provide light and ventilation.

The well-considered location of the various items of furniture makes the best possible use of the space.

A podium forms a relaxation area.

LIGHT FACTORY

The Light Factory used to house a bulb manufacturers. Part of it presented the present occupiers with the challenge of making a long, narrow space suitable to live in. By introducing several volumes, not only was storage space created, but its spatiality also remained intact. A raised podium forms a relaxation area. Steps lead to the basement containing the bedroom and bathroom. Concrete, steel and walnut give it all that distinct loft feeling.

Steps in steel and walnut lead to the raised living space.

The bathroom is frugal in design.

A variety of volumes are used as storage cupboards.

The bedroom is in the basement.

COMMERCIAL PREMISES

Lofts are increasingly being fitted out as commercial premises.
There are good reasons to do so.
The availability of a large floor area is of course important,
but the charm of a loft also gives extra prestige
to advertising and architects' offices,
or a designers' centre.

The chapel's neo-gothic arches are in sharp contrast to the watchtower cum television room
and the mobile documentation room cum library.
Several desks are hidden behind a long hedge of artificial leaves and a garden gate.

WHERE EVEN THE CLIENT
IS ONE OF THE FAMILY

To astonish everyone: that is the aim of the Kessels & Kramer advertising
agency. Whether it be with their work, their clients or their office.
The office is housed in an 1882 neo-gothic monastery chapel which,
after conversion, primarily radiates humour and originality.

The chapel houses a working area without walls, but with wooden forts,
a diving board, artificial grass and picnic tables.

Behind the fence there is a beach tower whose light-blue diving board invites one to a dip in the depths.

The imposing organ is still in working order, to the great delight of the employees and the great consternation of the neighbours.

A gothic church in all its glory.

Some of the desks and also the computers and of course the fake grass are green.

The ceiling arches are also lime-green, specially chosen to match the gold of the columns and the metal fans.

Work here is carried on in a shipping container in an old shed on an industrial estate.

The entrance is enough to tell you what to expect.

The shed has been kept intact.
Everything that can be touched has been given a coat of paint or is clad in metal.

Models on simple stands are on show in the middle of the shed.

DESIGN IN SHIPPING CONTAINERS

What do you do when your architects' office bursts its seams? You look for a solution that both offers more space and is representative of the style of your work. This is what MVS found on the Stork industrial estate.

The crude shed where machines used to be repaired now houses about thirty employees. The offices are in blue shipping containers so that each one has their own enclosed work-space. The other half of the shed does not yet have any particular use, and serves as a meeting place and relaxation area.

AN OFFICE AS QUIET AS A CHURCH

The serene peace necessary for a moment of reflection in a church can also come in handy during working hours. This is why the owners of the Office advertising agency saw in this empty church the perfect opportunity to show their clients some creativity and to encourage it among their staff.

Despite thorough conversion led by the architect Georges Witteveen, the high stained glass windows, the enormous area of the floor and the plain form have been preserved.

Even more space has been created in this sun-drenched church with the help of open staircases, landings and floating spaces.

While from the outside it is unmistakably a straightforward Reformed church,
inside it is an austere and light office.
By means of a platform with glass walls, an extra room for meetings, waiting or reading has been made
next to the reception desk.

Although it's a hive of activity, it's never untidy.
Everything has its place and function.

This bare church has become a superb place to work.

The creation of a void has linked the four storeys together visually.

*Account was also taken of the original architecture
when the four column-windows were cut out of the façade.*

WAREHOUSE 'PAKHUIS AMSTERDAM'

The Amsterdam Warehouse, completed in 1885, used to be part of a complex of three buildings called
Europe, Africa and Asia. The former Asia building, located on the Eastern commercial dock, part of the
IJ shore project, has been transformed into a contemporary design centre.

   As far as is known, this warehouse was always used for sugar and cacao. When the new owners took a
look in 1996, the bales of cacao were still stacked high. European furniture manufacturers and
importers now have their showrooms here.

The walls, wooden beam ceilings and cast-iron pillars have been retained.

The exhibitors are all under one roof, without clear divisions, but each has its own style.

On each floor there are four passageways
in the form of glass staircases or voids.

COLLECTORS

Works of art by the residents themselves,
antique objects, a glass case full of precious jewellery,
African masks, gloves, cutlery, odds and ends from jumble sales,
a collection of glassware, doorknobs,
there is nothing too odd to be a collector's item.
A loft does full justice to these objects
because they can be displayed so easily.

Unplastered walls to preserve the building's authenticity, a simple floor to emphasise its spaciousness and an unmodified beam structure for atmosphere and depth.

Top: *De Appel warehouse, as the present owner found it in 1971.*
Below: *The warehouse in a photo from 1900.*

WHERE HISTORY IS ALIVE

The oldest title deeds date from 1711, but De Appel warehouse was probably built sometime round 1660. Its present occupant, one of the city's first loft-dwellers, bought it from the Amsterdam Tobacco Company in the seventies and converted it into a wonderful loft full of original elements. The floors and ceilings, ventilation hatches and loading doors keep its history alive. It is striking that the full length of thirty metres has been maintained, while most of the other warehouses in the area have been divided in two.

Adzed beams also dominate the bedroom.

The intimate grey corner, set below the beam-line, is complete with open fireplace.

The dining area is exactly in the middle of the warehouse, with the library and bedroom above it.

The aluminium-clad library and the industrial piping against the ceiling contrast sharply
with the antique furniture and the classical art. This is a combination that makes for plenty of surprises throughout the loft.
Colour is not avoided anywhere. Striking colour combinations liven up one corner after another.

A VENETIAN PALAZZO

In a former coach-house built in 1880, a three hundred square metre loft has with great imagination been transformed into a Venetian *palazzo*. Sizeable works of art, imposing statues and delicate objects are to be found everywhere in this home. The occupant clearly loves classical and southern elements.

    This emphasises the creative use of colour and the humorous murals also establish a thoroughly theatrical feel.

The oval library can be completely closed off using sliding walls.

*Time stands still in this library and the owner can browse
through the extensive collection of art books in perfect peace.*

The mural is a modified copy of a work by the Italian artist Tiepolo.

The deep-blue painted kitchen is in the exact centre of the space.

The original supporting pillars are integrated into the decor.

Superb works of art create a subdued atmosphere.

The Rhonda Zwillinger toy soldier stands guard.

The sitting area with the Le Corbusier chairs forms a corner separate from the rest of the loft.

IN A COLONIAL ATMOSPHERE

In one of the many warehouses with which Amsterdam is blessed, a loft was created where relaxation and comfort come top of the list. Together with the restrained use of colours, the open kitchen, white columns and the ingenious differences in level give the impression of space. Wood, in combination with objects from all over the world, establishes a colonial atmosphere.

Books from floor to ceiling. The ideal background for the television and reading area.

The bathroom is bright with refined wood-coloured and black accents.

The upper storey is still completely intact. Even the seventeenth-century wooden floor is authentic.
The only division in the otherwise open space is a large glass case.

SUGAR-SWEET ROMANTICISM

A seventeenth-century sugar warehouse in the charming Jordaan was named after Mercury, the god of trade. Cane sugar and syrup were stored there in large earthenware pots. For this reason the warehouse had to be built entirely in brick and reinforced with extra beams so that the wooden floors could support this heavy load.

All this is still clear to see in this romantic loft filled with antique furniture, retro-objects and all manner of curios.

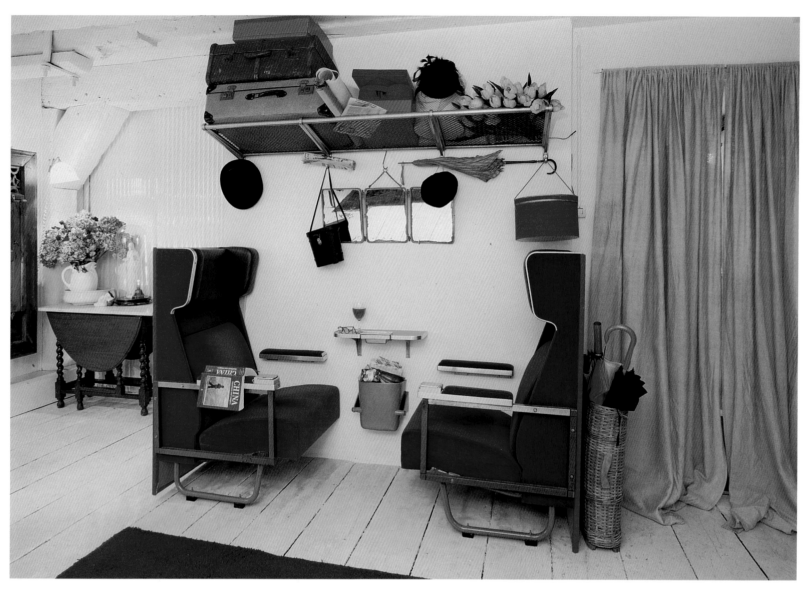

The first thing that strikes one on entering is the interior of a second-class train compartment complete with suitcases and books.

One bedroom has been made in the large space on the canal side.

Soft furnishings in old rose and antique furniture create a romantic atmosphere.

Old cinema seats and Brussels theatre lamps; the unique atmosphere of the past is present everywhere in this loft.

The rough floor in hardwood from the Philippines, formerly much used for gymnasiums, contrasts sharply with the smooth, dark ceiling.

The design of the interior is full of contrasts too, with a smooth transition from modern to classical.

Classical objects like the big gilt mirror, the church candelabrum and the stately portraits
are perfect complements to the red sofa.

ANTIQUE MODERNISM

A vigorous combination of exceptional antique objects with contemporary
art and design plays a strong hand here. The plain shades of the walls, floor,
ceiling, furniture and open fireplace, perfectly attuned to one another,
are interrupted only by sculptures and paintings in bright colours.
This occupant clearly does not prefer a single style or period, but simply
beauty. The front is dominated by big high windows subdivided in the
classicist manner, which allows plenty of light in.

This even gives the unworked floor a vivid gleam.

Simplicity is a virtue. Simple forms, restrained colours and the open fireplace clad in steel provide serenity.

Despite the great size of the bedroom, the open bathroom with its freestanding bathtub dominates the space.

In the dining area near the open kitchen, a long sturdy table has been chosen, with Arne Jacobsen's 'Triennale' chairs in black and white.

The white-painted roof structure spans the living and sleeping area like a clear sky above their colonial atmosphere.

The bath is ingeniously hidden away behind cupboard doors.

NARDA'S ARK

Two storeys in an old school, making two hundred sixty five square metres in all. Life here goes on amongst dozens of photos and souvenirs of distant travels. The light enters freely through the many windows in the kitchen *cum* dining room. The large living area under the roof ridge is very special because of the wooden roof structure, which is built on the principle of an upturned ship's hull. Homely cosiness down below and adventurous jungle scenes up above.

*A still-life has been created with works by various photographers,
next to a painting by Klaas Gubbels on the wall in a corner of the kitchen.*

Africa and other remote continents are never far away.

The preponderant white and the old chestnut floor, with the addition of a copious collection of travel objects, gives the whole space a warm distinction.

Small well-loved objects and belongings are lying or standing everywhere you look. Silver candlesticks and glass bells, pots and pans, nothing is hidden away. Everything is within easy reach or in open wall cabinets.

The atmosphere is defined by the black and white floor, the full-length arched windows, the open cabinets and the long table with its comfortable Thonet chairs.

In the well-lit space in the rear building the former employees of the bank sat at their desks processing data.

Now it is a large room in a splendid combination of austerity and nonchalance.

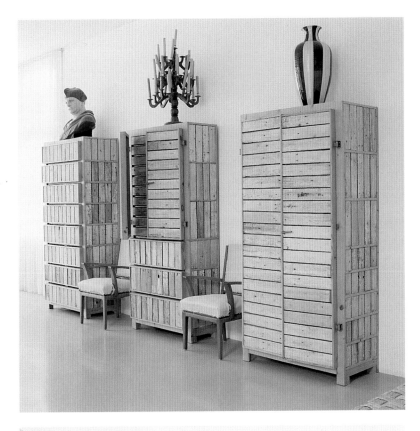

In the big room there are three cabinets by Piet Hein Eek.

The occupant chose to have a moveable bedroom.

Drawers and recesses make this simple wall into a proper piece of furniture.

A MARVELLOUS WORLD IN AN OLD BANK BUILDING

This old bank building with the stylish offices of the former management, equipped with impressive Lips safes, was transformed into a magnificent loft with two separate atmospheres. Baroque and theatrical on one side of the corridor, functional and minimalist on the other.

What immediately strikes one about the bathroom is the extreme symmetry and the timeless accessories.

An extensive collection of African masks hangs above the long, high kitchen unit.
The way they are hung for display makes them into a single work of art.

All the cabinets have wheels so they can always be arranged differently.

*In the prestigious period room at the front, the former bank manager's office,
the collection of 'Classical and Baroque' now has a fitting home.*

Part of the collection of self-designed cushions is lying in the Biedermeier chair.

Two imposing Lips safes are to be found behind heavy wooden doors.

Home concerts around the Bösendorfer grand seat a select audience of a hundred and fifty.

The modern kitchen with no less than five ovens perfectly matches the style of the house.

A bronze revolving door grabs one's attention in the impressive entrance hall.

THE GOOD SAMARITAN

An area of one thousand five hundred fifty square metres cannot be designed at a single stroke.

In fact the occupants took more than four years to arrange the whole space according to their taste and views.

The showpiece of the house is the superb hundred twenty square metre Jugendstil entrance hall. The beautiful decoration of the living area exudes immense peace and warmth because everything has been made in accordance with the golden section. No trouble was too great when it came to decorating this building: handwoven silk curtains and wall-coverings from Florence, a hand-blown Murano chandelier, a Bösendorfer grand piano like a virtuoso beacon in the middle of the living area, and also marvellous antique objects including the painting *The Good Samaritan* by Terwesten, a contemporary of Rembrandt.

The whole interior radiates restfulness and class.

*The occupants work on their condition in the swimming pool
eight metres under the Amsterdam ordnance datum.*

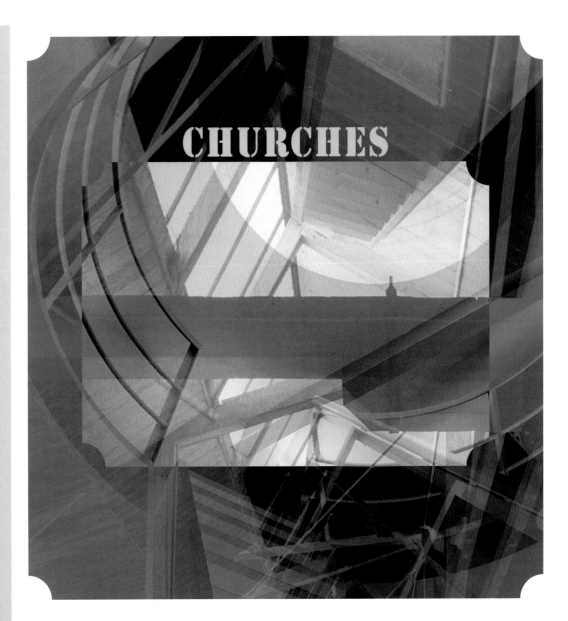

CHURCHES

Living in a church?
It used to raise eyebrows, but now it's thought perfectly normal.
Partly as a result of the fall in church attendance,
there are a great many vacant places of worship in Amsterdam.
Their unusual layout
and often interesting architecture
present a particular attraction to loft-dwellers.

The church windows and the carpentry of the ceiling are breathtaking.
The iron rods on which the church lamps hung can still be clearly seen under the ridge of the roof.
The woodwork is in three shades of grey which merge into one another in a wave pattern.
This is how it was and this is how it will stay.

SHELTER IN A CHURCH

This former 17th-century brewery is bursting with history. In fact it has had different owners every century. At one stage it was occupied by Anabaptists who worshipped there in secret. They converted it into one great shelter, complete with a central aisle, two apses and a double gallery on the first floor.

At a later date an auction house found it a good home, until it too moved all its goods and chattels and an adventurous new occupant saw her chance to create a superb home with an entirely unique character. All the original dimensions, windows and colours have been preserved.

Cushions, throws and an abundance of small accessories give this large space an intimate atmosphere.

Only a small part of this shelter has been sacrificed to such functional rooms as bedrooms and bathroom.

A small but cosy roof terrace means it is possible to enjoy every ray of sun.

The kitchen is cool, modern and functional. Behind it is a spacious larder with a goods lift.

The owners have a splendid view of the kitchen from a void that leads to the terrace.

'IMPS & ELFS' OVER THE FONT

In close collaboration with the architect Jaap Dijkman, the immense area of the former Pro Rege Chapel was converted into a fantastic space in which to live and work. In the front part of the church, formerly the deacons and district nurses' sections, are now the offices and design studio of the 'Imps & Elfs' baby and children's company. The rear part, formerly a toddlers' playroom, now contains the bathroom and bedrooms.
The enormous chapel space is perfect for cooking, relaxing, reading and playing, every aspect of a pleasant life.

The structure of the church has been preserved.
A notable feature is the large arch with a motto and the round window under the ridge.
A mezzanine has been built above the kitchen, across the whole width of the façade.
This gives the kitchen a practical intimacy and breaks the tremendous height.

The organ used to stand behind the large window, but now there is a big desk for working on the items in the collection.

This cooking area with the air of a catering kitchen is ideal for receiving guests.

The dark mahogany of the old pews has been reused not only in the kitchen but also in the bathroom.
The chestnut floor matches the light colours of the sitting area perfectly.

The immense archive cabinet stands in the space like a wall.

The sturdy table, an heirloom, is proudly displayed in a recess in the kitchen.

The restored stained glass windows can be fully opened.

The maximum use of height and the large double glass doors bring light and space to the living room.
The two armchairs were made to measure, a large one for him and a smaller one for her.

PLAIN LUXURY

In a quiet green district, this former Reformed church now houses an
unusual loft with plenty of privacy and an atmosphere all its own.
The original detailing of the church, like the beams, doors and windows
have as far as possible been retained. Such luxurious functional additions as
open hearths, voids and a marvellous swimming pool provide maximum
comfort in a minimal setting. Modern interior design is effortlessly
combined with antique furniture and restored heirlooms, which gives one
corner the look of a mediaeval castle and the other that of a chic spa.

The original robust brick walls inlaid with a yellow-green tiled edging appear throughout the loft.

A generous swimming pool has been built in the cellar, accessible via an original round-arched church door.

The atmosphere of the church is still palpable in the air of the communal entrance hall.

The entire structure of the former synagogue was preserved.

The kitchen design includes a mobile work-block.

'A LAMP IS THE PRAYER, THE LAW A LIGHT'

This Dutch proverb is of great relevance to this 1913 synagogue. At that time they probably never thought it would one day be used as a home. Many of the elements introduced by the architect, Elte, are closely linked to the restrained style of the well-known Dutch architect Berlage. The present occupants were immediately taken with the unusually large area and its character. The two floors were divided in a practical way. The bedrooms and bathrooms are downstairs, while upstairs the loft principle was maintained by the openness of the kitchen and living room. This space speaks for itself. The conversion produced a surprise too - under the house is a vaulted cellar where the women used to have their ritual bath.

It has not yet been decided to what new use it will be put.

The red wall brings colour and warmth to the bedroom.

The ground floor includes the children's room, bathrooms and the main bedroom.

The glass walls round the bedroom create a floating effect.

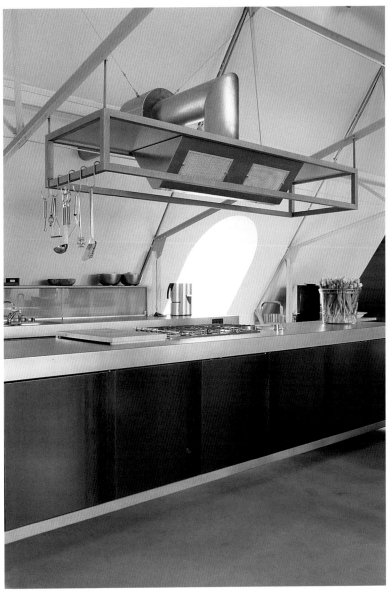

The big extractor gives the kitchen an industrial look.

A HEAVENLY HOME

Surprisingly enough, one of the finest lofts in Amsterdam is not in an industrial setting. What is more, this home has been created on holy ground. The tremendous height and characteristic form of the Reformed church were a challenge to the architect George Witteveen. Creativity and boldness were essential. What most catches the eye is the big bedroom seemingly floating in the air, surrounded by glass and with a concrete bed in the middle. This loft radiates openness. Other notable features are the white-oiled wood, the untreated beams and a scoured concrete floor. A variety of materials is used: walls of steel sheeting, cupboards clad in copper sheeting and sandblasted glass.

The open dressing room on the landing looks out at the restored church window
that is one of the few items preserved from the place of worship.

Glass has been installed between the rafters to make enormous windows.
Weather permitting, they can be opened and then it is like being outdoors.

The platform in white-oiled wood visually separates the dining room from the living area.
The various shades of red and lilac in the children's room exudes a fairytale warmth.

A floating staircase leads from the simple bathroom to the master bedroom.
The shallow washbasin is very unusual.

The abundant use of natural materials creates an austere impression.

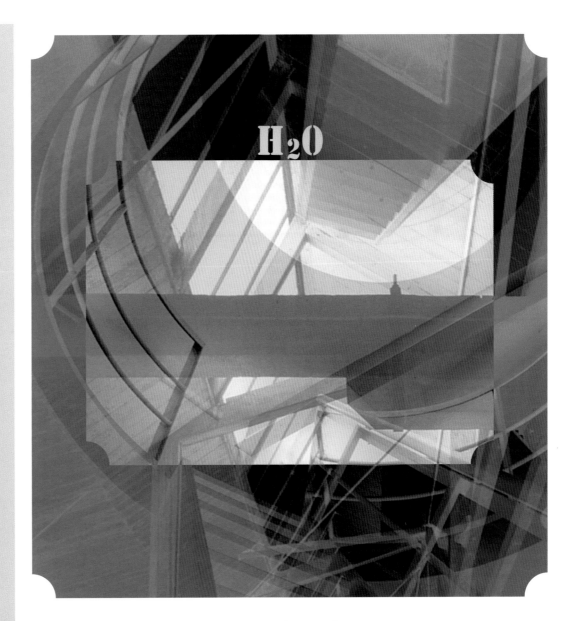

H₂O

Say Amsterdam,
and you immediately think of its famous canals,
alongside which most of the former merchants' houses were built.
The proximity of water makes it an even greater pleasure
to live in a loft.
Anyone who loves space and water
will find the perfect home in the old port area with a view of the IJ.

The kitchen is well tucked away behind a wall, allowing plenty of space for the sitting areas.

EMMA'S ISLAND

In 1909, the Emma warehouse on the distinctive Prinseneiland only had two storeys. Two more were added in 1930. Today, the four storeys, with a total floor area of nine hundred square metres, are occupied by a single family. The living area at the top has the atmosphere of an American penthouse, with a fine roof terrace overlooking the water. The floor beneath houses the work room, bedrooms and bathrooms. Down below it is possible to open a water-gate to allow a boat to sail in.

In the austere hall one imagines oneself in an American building of the thirties.

Symmetry is provided by the furniture at the brick open fireplace with its steel tray.

On the first floor, everything is still as the present owner found it. A multifunctional space that can be divided and fitted out exactly as desired.

The intimate roof terrace, continuing the line of the living room, is concealed behind the original façade.

A glass wall divides the studio from the living quarters.

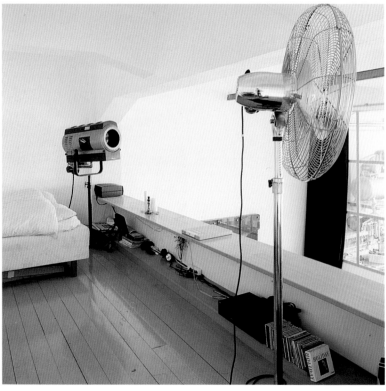

At the rear of the building is a mezzanine that functions as a bedroom.

The artist's colossal sculptures are regularly exhibited here.
The hoists on the ceiling enable heavy materials to be moved about.

ON THE WATERSIDE OF THE WORLD

As the sculptor Mathieu Nab himself puts it, with his broad view over the IJ, he has a place on the waterside of the world. This old warehouse in the port, with its solid foundations and great load-bearing capacity, is the ideal setting for his studio. He brings heavy blocks of marble and loads of timber in with a fork-lift truck. The goldsmith Anouchka Verhagen also has her workplace here, where she makes exclusive rings and jewels. The building is also perfect for exhibitions, receptions and parties. But the occupiers are not entirely happy with the renovation of the old warehouses. They mainly mourn the loss of the sturdy wooden doors and the pursuit of uniformity.

Although the Lofra's *mooring is in the eastern port of Amsterdam,*
the 'bargees' still regularly set sail.

Virtually all the original parts of the barge were preserved,
including the wooden floor.

WELCOME ON BOARD

The *Lofra* is a Belgian barge built in 1963 which was put to new use several years ago. This houseboat, thirty-nine metres long and five wide, has the air of a ballroom and adheres to the loft concept.

It is no surprise that parties for more than a hundred guests are regularly organised. There are specific problems in converting a barge. No less than thirty tons of concrete blocks were needed at several points to ensure stability. As the *Lofra* still regularly sets sail, all the utilities had to be duplicated: gas and oil, 220 and 24 volts, a watertank on board and water supply from the bank. The barge also has to be put in dry-dock every four years to tar its steel bottom.

The bathroom was installed in a cube standing free from the sides of the barge.

The kitchen is at the front of the barge for practical reasons.

The original sliding panels always allow sufficient light into the kitchen.

The kitchen and living room are connected by steps.

From the bedroom, the occupants can look out over the water through authentic round portholes.

Now it is weathered, the house fits in perfectly with the rest of the small warehouses and yards that line Prinseneiland, and seems to have been there for centuries.

The colours have been meticulously selected: Amsterdam canal red for the accents, sky blue for the ceiling and beige for the floor, as if it were scattered with sand. A house for outdoor people, in the heart of Amsterdam.

BOATBUILDER BECOMES LOFT-BUILDER

Until very recently, there stood a sixteenth-century warehouse on Prinseneiland that formed part of a shipyard, and now a wooden building has once again been erected on this site. The boatbuilder and designer Wouter Nieuwveld, together with his wife and two children, thought he would like a house on the waterside, one with the same maritime and industrial character as before. It was to become an extraordinary building in brick, metal and wood, and from outside it really does resemble a boathouse, though inside it has the bright and spacious quality of a loft.

All the bedroom and bathroom doors that open onto the suspended landing
are identical and in fact resemble ship's cabins.

To make the holiday mood complete, space has been made for a swimming pool.

Washing can be hoisted up and down by means of a sturdy pulley system.

The lamp fixed to the ceiling by the tie-bars comes originally from the station at Flushing.

FROM JUGENDSTIL

TO MINIMALISM

Loft-dwellers are not usually great friends
of banality, excessive uniformity or predictability.
Their interiors are often a reflection
of the dynamism of their own lives.
The ingenious use of colour and light,
playing off hard and soft and warm and cold
against each other can enable a loft to grow
into an exceptional home of thoroughly original design.

The load-bearing pillars are a sign of the loft's industrial past.

The open kitchen is at one with the living room.

GIETERSHOF

An old factory in Jordaan, squatted by artists years ago, has now become the Gietershof, comprising forty dwellings. As well as the aged and weathered wooden beams, the original load-bearing pillars make an immediate impression. From the living room with open kitchen there is a view of the enclosed communal garden.

Two architects were appointed for this project, which presented the residents with diverse ideas and later enabled them to make a choice. For this conversion, the architects had the very practical idea of making a large-scale model giving a realistic notion of the future dwellings.

The windows in the living room provide plentiful natural light.

One of the loft's most outstanding features
is the original beam construction.

*The glass wall forms a natural transition
between the living room and the bathroom.*

The bath with its wrought iron legs is a retro element in the bathroom.

The table and bench can be folded in to leave a clearer passage to the kitchen.

A RAY OF SUNSHINE IN THE HOUSE

A bright and open loft has been created in a building that used to house the Ziekenfonds [health insurance fund]. The use of cheerful colours, mainly shades of red, green and blue, make this a sunny home. Spaciousness has been created by continuing the balustrade around and down the entire stairwell. This extended the open structure downwards.

The yellow wall that hides the kitchen is in unison with the original dining area.

The bedrooms and bathrooms are downstairs, as is a library cum television room.

The comical sculpture is by the artist Ripolles.

Stairs in the middle of the room lead to the upper floor.
Glass roof panels let in a mass of light.

THAT ORANGE FEELING

The occupiers of this loft cannot be accused of Dutch chauvinism – they only chose orange for the large partition walls in the living area because of its warmth. This is a building with a full history.

Carpenters held their trade union meetings there, the Nazis requisitioned the building as their headquarters and after that came a company making pick-up needles. Most architectural elements have been preserved, such as the authentic steel windows, iron trusses and glass roof panels that allow in abundant light. The neighbourhood is not the most popular residential area in Amsterdam, but the charm of the building and its spacious roof terrace thoroughly make up for that. The children are mad about the loft. They clamber up the ropes, swing for hours or let themselves go on a punchball.

The open kitchen fits in perfectly with the rest of the living area.

A fine roof terrace adds a touch of luxury.

Like the bedrooms, the bathroom is separated from the living area.

Nothing diverts the attention. The sitting area is adorned by nothing more than a comfortable sofa and an extendable coffee table.

LOFT WITH ALLURE

Away with colour, away with superfluous objects that will get in the way.
In the architect Jen Alkema's minimalist loft everything revolves around space, light and emptiness. The result is a refreshing contemporary space that fits surprisingly well into the stately old grandeur of its surroundings. The high ceiling in the mostly white living area creates a tremendous clearness. Clear transitions in the form of steps or a void lead to other rooms. The form and function of the simple furniture are of prime importance.

The living area is reached via a landing higher up.
A long bookcase has been built in under the balustrade.

The large balcony with its old-fashioned landing give the loft a royal air.

The austere white kitchen acts as the passageway from the living room to the other rooms.

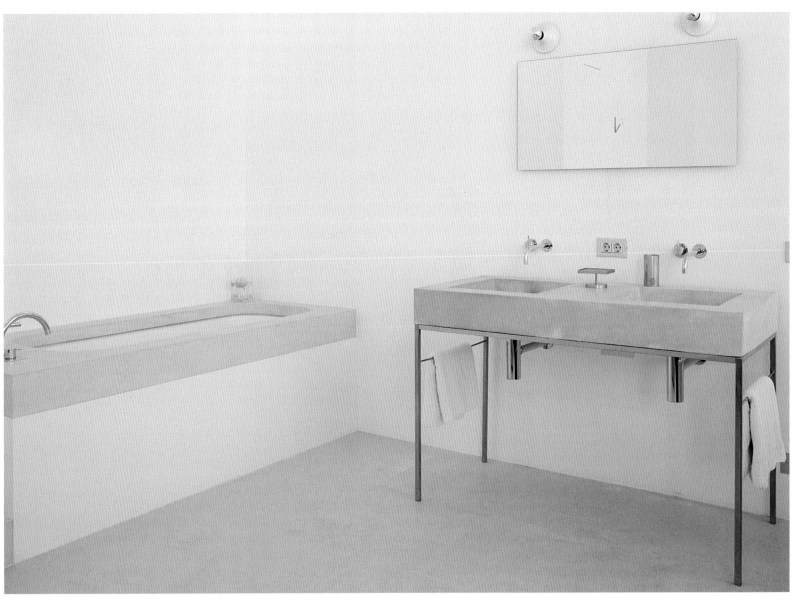

In the bathroom limestone has been used in combination with stainless steel.

*Moveable cubes and chairs found on a scrapheap
are used as a long dining and reading table.*

Iron cupboards from KLM are used as kitchen cabinets.

On the wall there is a replica of 'Tarzan with a spear' in a zinc-like material.

ONE-ARM BANDITS

In the past, gambling machines, commonly called one-arm bandits, were manufactured here. The building, with its host of compartments and rooms, was converted piece by piece into a proper loft with plenty of space. Blue, red and green give it a Mediterranean atmosphere.

The decor has the air of a curiosity shop. Its inspiration is drawn from found objects and treasure hunts amongst the rubbish. Iron cupboards from KLM serve as kitchen cabinets, and a buck from a gym now provides the base for a work of art. Other eye-catchers include window-dressing material from the Bijenkorf department store and an old lamp from the Olympic stadium.

The occupier has incorporated the names of cars from his youth into a work of art. A notable feature is the extensive collection of 'design in printed matter', from books in the form of a box to one-off editions in inflatable plastic.

A wooden frame gives the mirror a playful touch.

The work of art above the fire is something the owner just found amongst the household rubbish on the street.

The bathroom adjoins the bedroom.

A shop-window display from the Bijenkorf department store is now a work of art.

The striking mirror is from a design by Gaudi.

The open kitchen runs on from the living room so as to retain its spaciousness.

The oval cherry-wood table is completely integrated into the living area.

'T BLAEUWE HUYS

't Blaeuwe Huys is the name of a seventeenth-century building on the Herengracht, designed by the Belgian architect Hans Rombouts. It now contains seventeen flats. For a long time it housed a bank, and the authentic evidence of this is seen in the revolving door and the waiting room with its counters. The people in the loft on the ground floor have arranged their interior bit by bit. White is the dominant colour, while a red wall in the dining room provides a warm tint. The kitchen has a large round window that looks into the children's room. This patio in the middle of the city is seen as a piece of priceless luxury.

This load-bearing column is one of the remnants of the original building.

Piano recitals are given regularly in this magnificent hall.

The patio is one of the residents' favourite spots.

The blocks on the bath were glued with silicon to form a squared glass wall.

All the doors are three metres high.

The kitchen wall has been chiselled off for warmth and originality.
Next to this there is even a part in concrete.

The design classics, like the Artifort chair, the sofa by Martin Visser and the Spectrum table with its inlaid Indian slate, are family heirlooms. The carpet, with the appropriate name of 'Stone', and the lino floor are part of this New Realism.

COLOURED GREY

In his own loft, the interior designer Paul Alexander Linse's views on living in a space have led to its functional and minimalist character. The stairwell has been demolished completely to gain space, the walls have been chiselled and roughly plastered, the doors are endlessly high and the grey floor has no skirting. This gives the liberating feeling that everything runs on and can always change. Grey is the dominant colour, one which enforces restfulness. Whether it be the floor, a carpet or the kitchen.

COLOUR GALORE

The loft owned by the architect and urban designer Sjoerd Soeters
is well-known in Amsterdam and beyond. This former school building is in
a daring pink with eye-catching graceful white woodwork. Inside, the large
colourful space is full of design pieces, including proven classics and striking
new ones. They are scattered throughout the living, kitchen and bedroom
areas, which are linked together by means of voids, suspended floors and
glazed corridors.

Where does one look first?
High cupboards, a Murano glass lamp and floating rooms all
conspire to stimulate the mind.
Above the sitting area hangs the guestroom
screened off with canvas.

In the green and white bathroom the unusual pattern of the large tiles brings to life a superb play of lines.

Meals are enjoyed in the frivolous curve of the overhanging void.

There is not a sign of cool design in this expressive home. The comfortable chairs are remakes of the English Howard chairs of the nineteenth century. The lightweight tables standing amongst the seats are by Zanotta and the white lamps were designed by Rizzatto.

African motifs provide atmospheric tints in the living room.

A free-standing work-block is the centrepiece of the kitchen.

Oregon pine was chosen to give the living room a warm parquet floor.

AFRICA BLUES

In the sixteenth century this building housed a dye-works, and much later it was home to several schools. Now, in 2000, part of this canal-side house has been turned into a colourful, lively loft.

There is an abundance of space, so that the children were able to learn to ride a bike in the living room. The variety of her work as a stylist leads Inger Kolff to change the decor regularly. After a time in Mali she acquired a taste for all things African.

The brilliant colours of the cloths, fabrics and various objects bring the continent to life right here in Amsterdam. And to top it all, there is a sheltered roof terrace, where the flowers and plants are watered by a computerised system.

A semicircular oak screen divides the kitchen from the dining room.

The industrial staircase to the upper floor was specially made by a smith.

The roof terrace is the owners' favourite spot in fine weather.

Flower arrangements also fit perfectly into the loft's lively decoration.

The purple wall is the first thing that strikes you on entering the bathroom.

In addition to the owners' own inspiration, various artists' work also gives the loft added colour.

The landing was the perfect place to hang an indoor swing for the children.

The inhabitants chose to enjoy the space to the maximum,
as can be seen in the dining room.

GREEN OASIS IN THE CITY CENTRE

A former depot for ship's equipment has been very tastefully transformed
by the present occupants into an atmospheric home. This classified building
was in very poor condition and exceedingly thorough renovation was
needed, in consultation with the Department of Monuments. A number of
original elements were nevertheless preserved, such as the cast-iron
windows. This loft is very comfortable and spacious. In addition, a green
oasis of at least two hundred square metres was created on the roof, which is
almost unique in Amsterdam city centre.

The open, transparent kitchen reinforces the spacious feeling of the loft.

The cedar staircase leads to the terrace.

A green roof terrace, three floors up, with pleached limes, mulberries and grapes.

The stairs are constructed in a tight rhythm:

the gaps between the lateral planks coincide with the treads.

In this loft one is struck by the heating pipes on the ceiling.

The stainless steel refrigerator in the kitchen and the use of deep, robust colours enhances its young, industrial quality.

A low bookcase runs along the wall from front to back.
It holds a collection of favourite drawings, paintings and photos.

SURPRISE CORNERS, STURDY ROOMS

Here we see a highly practical layout combined with all the advantages offered by a large space. Although each room has a character of its own, the kitchen, living, bath and bedroom actually flow seamlessly into one another. This loft's attraction lies in its various levels, the cheerful range of colours and the visible industrial elements.

A collection of vases makes for a colourful accent above the kitchen worktop.

A surprise lurks behind every wall.
In this way the living room, kitchen, bedroom and bathroom appear one after the other.

The glass walls screen the bedroom off from the bathroom and filters the light on both sides.

The double wooden doors with their frosted glass do not conceal a cupboard, but the entrance.

The different levels enable the space to be used to the maximum.

HOW PERCEPTION CAN MAKE SOMETHING SMALL INTO SOMETHING GRAND

A relatively small but very high attic floor has been converted so as to make it open, spacious and functional.

Landings, raised floors and openings in steel and wood together form a practical arrangement. Large windows have been set between the rafters, allowing plenty of light in and providing brightness and serenity.

Top: Cupboard space has been made in a cube next to the original loading bay.
The bedroom is mounted on top of it. The way to the bathroom is over the catwalk.

This singularly shaped fire is an exact copy of one Picasso had in his studio.

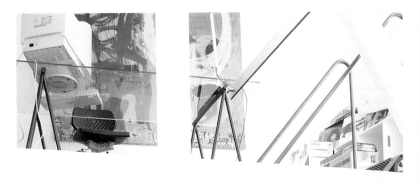

The steps on wheels can be moved right to the front.

The shower is nicely tucked away in a steel cage.

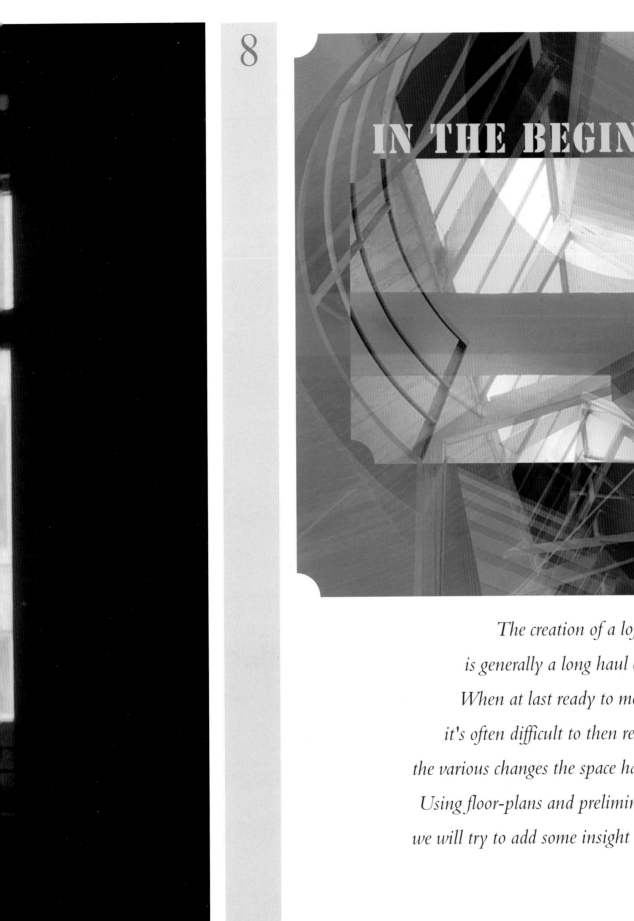

IN THE BEGINNING

The creation of a loft
is generally a long haul effort.
When at last ready to move in,
it's often difficult to then reconstruct
the various changes the space has undergone.
Using floor-plans and preliminary designs,
we will try to add some insight to the matter.

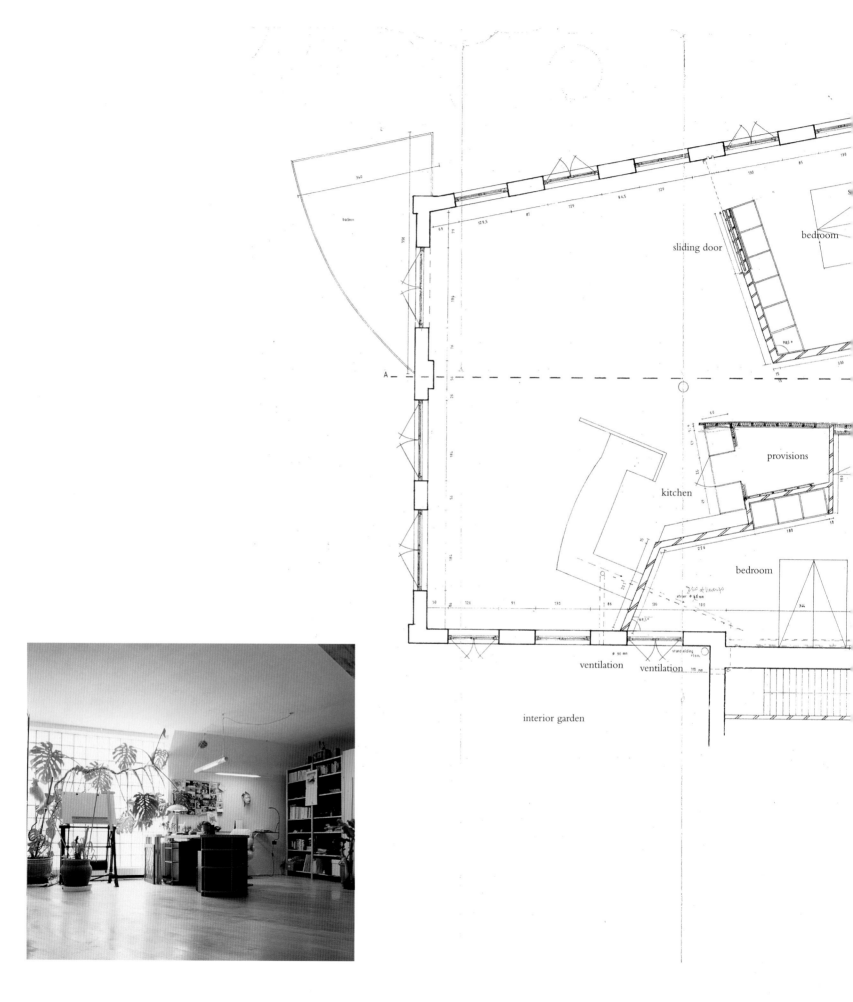

sliding door

bedroom

provisions

kitchen

bedroom

ventilation   ventilation

interior garden

A

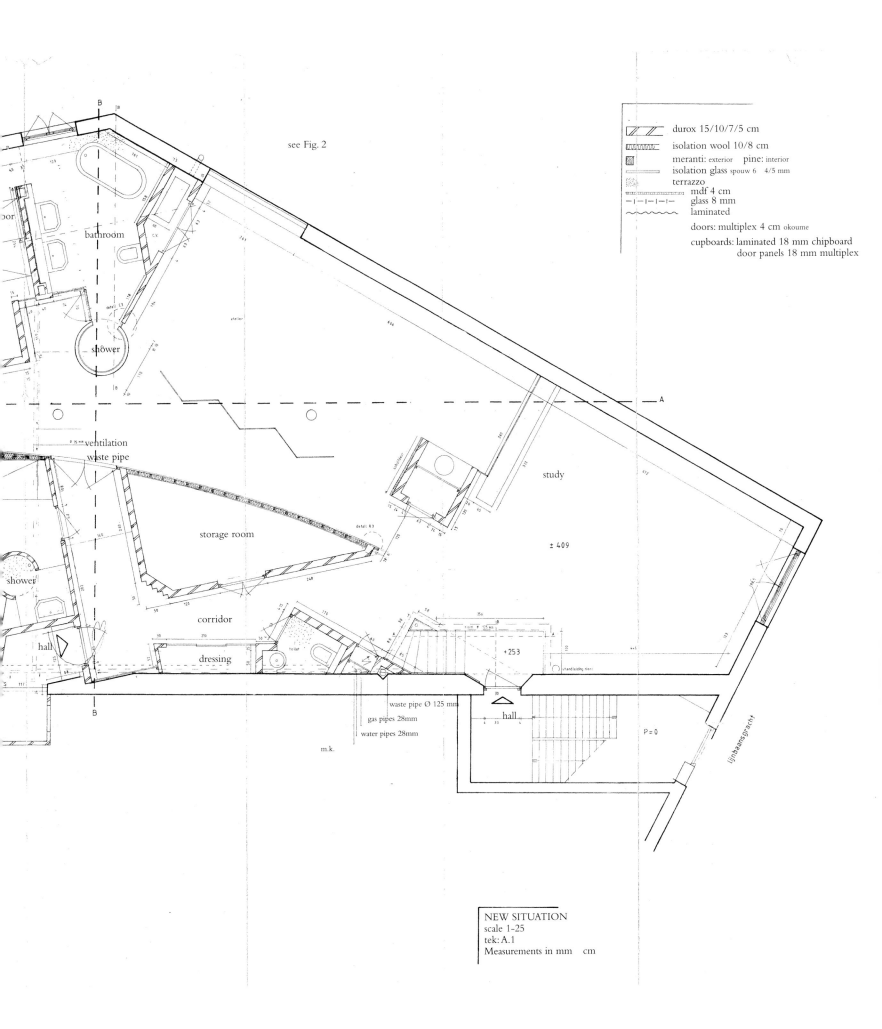

see Fig. 2

bathroom

shower

ventilation
waste pipe

shower

storage room

study

± 409

hall

corridor

dressing

hall

+ 253

waste pipe Ø 125 mm

gas pipes 28mm

water pipes 28mm

m.k.

P = 0

lijnbaansgracht

durox 15/10/7/5 cm
isolation wool 10/8 cm
meranti: exterior   pine: interior
isolation glass spouw 6   4/5 mm
terrazzo
mdf 4 cm
glass 8 mm
laminated
doors: multiplex 4 cm okoume
cupboards: laminated 18 mm chipboard
door panels 18 mm multiplex

NEW SITUATION
scale 1-25
tek: A.1
Measurements in mm   cm

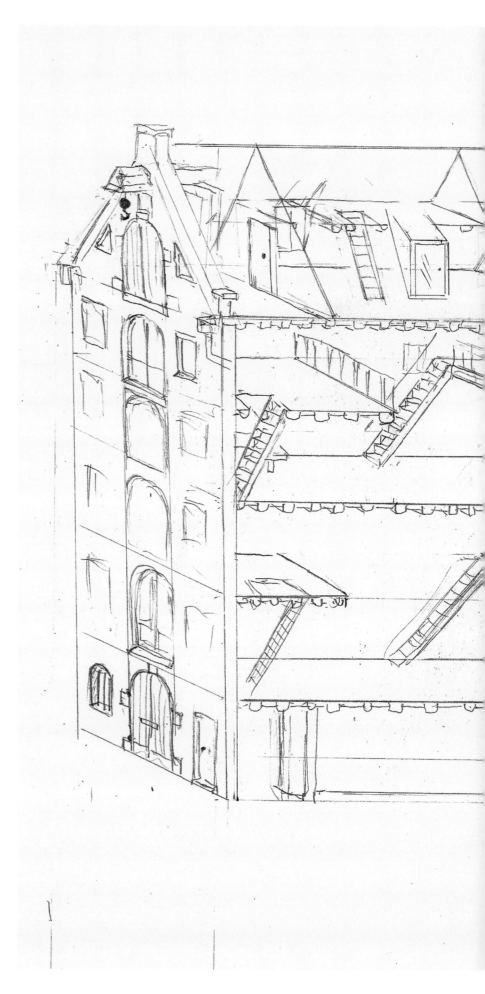

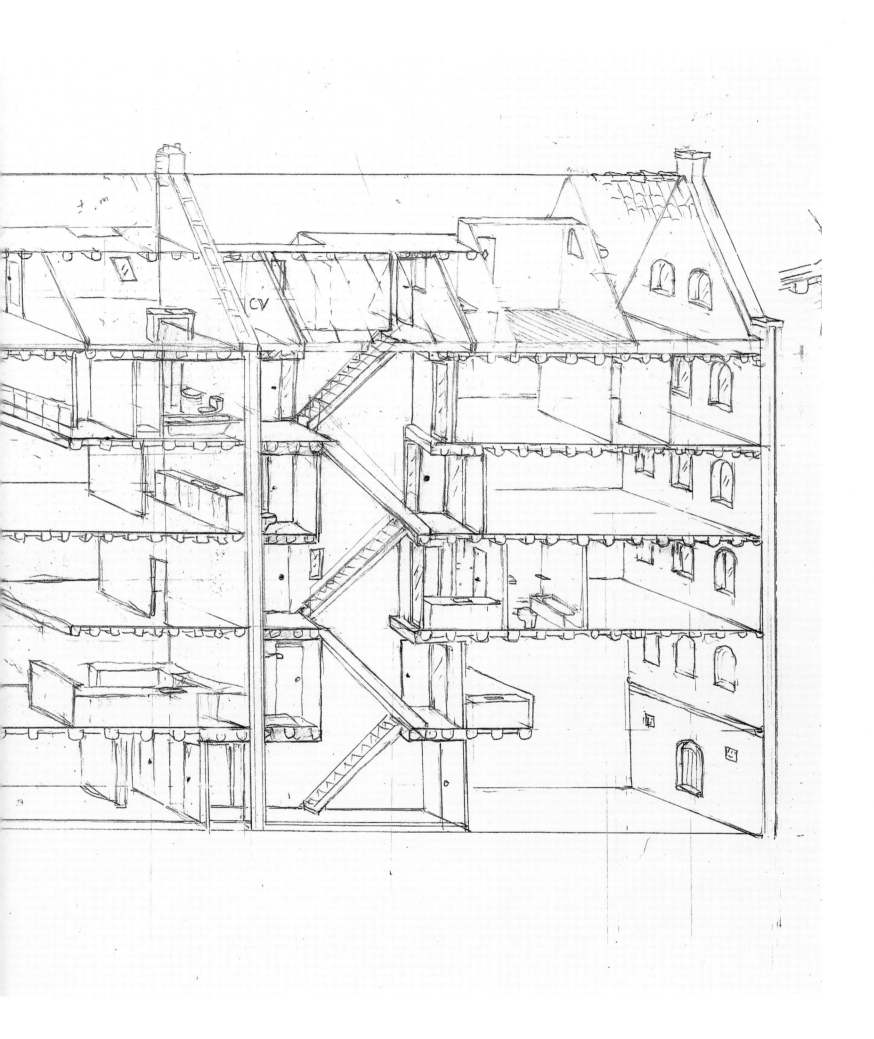

CV

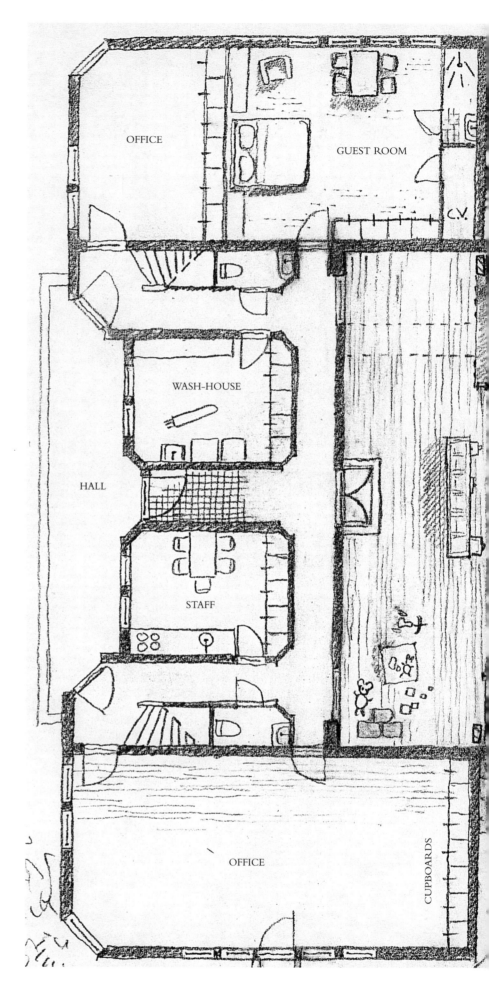

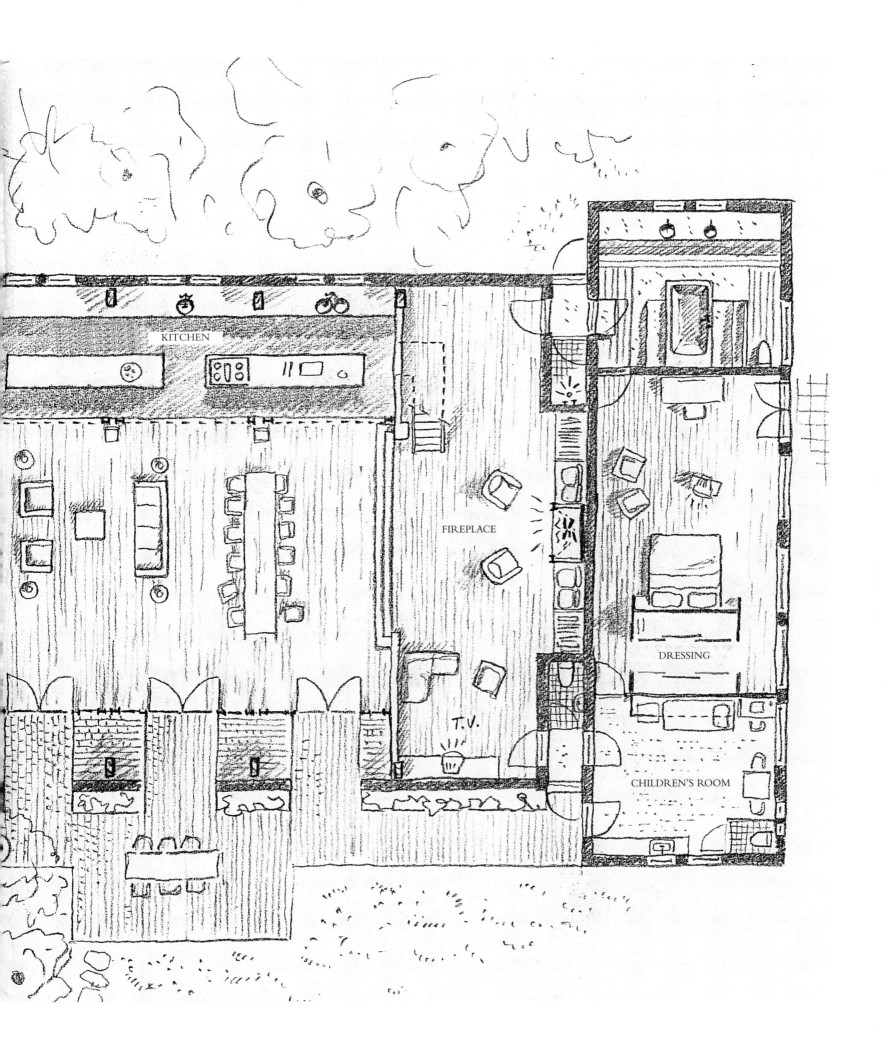

KITCHEN

FIREPLACE

T.V.

DRESSING

CHILDREN'S ROOM

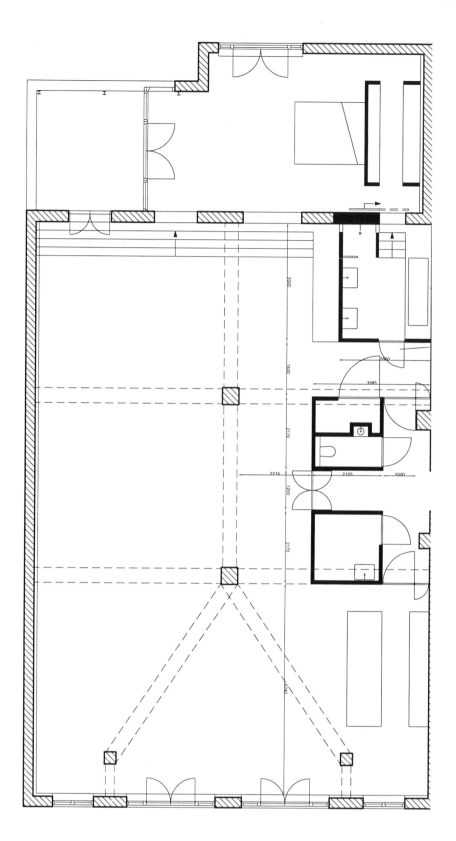

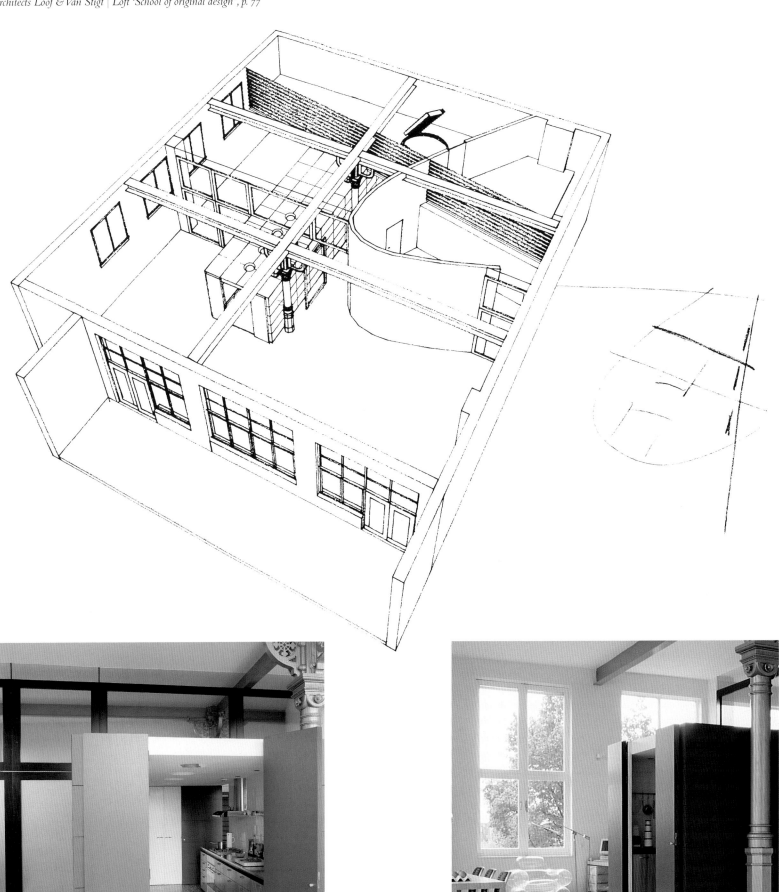

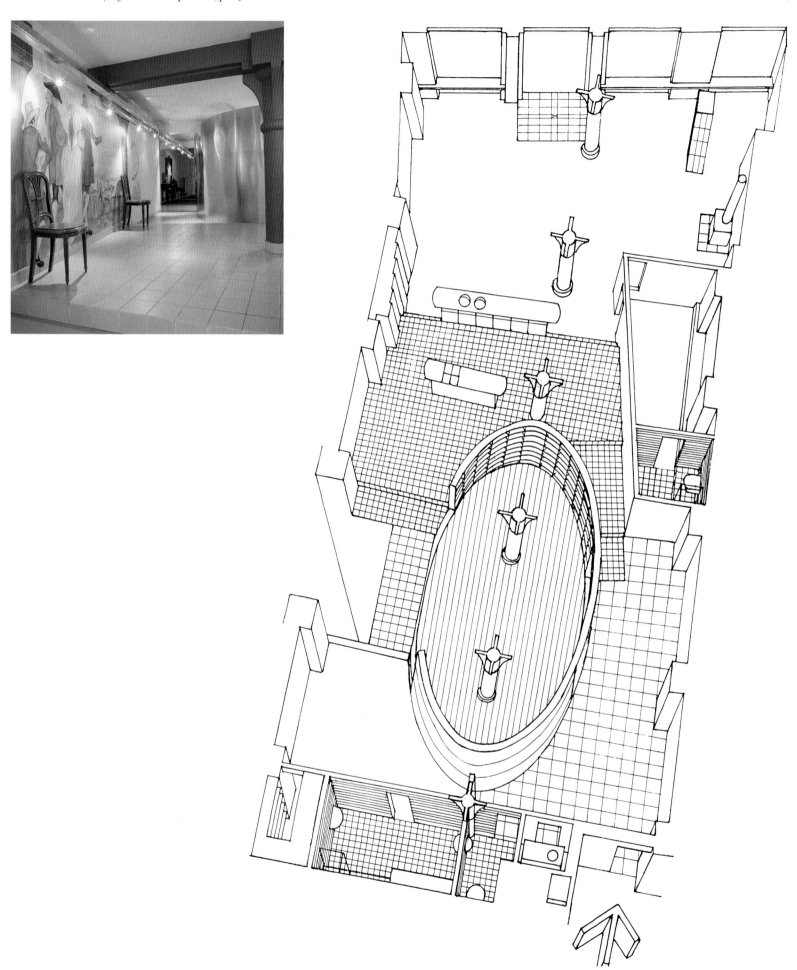

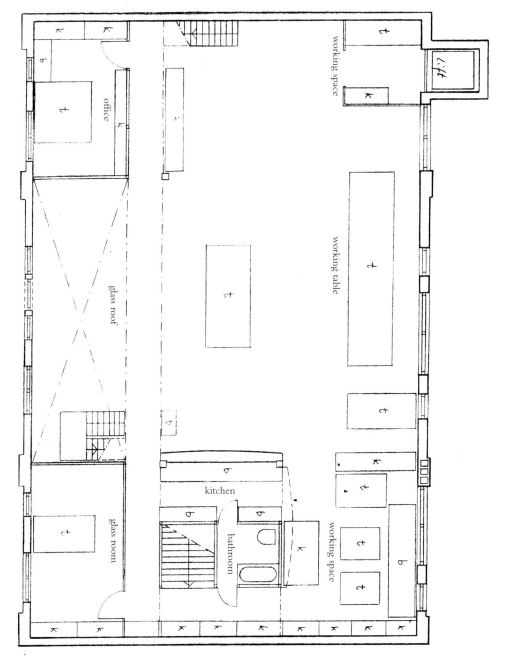

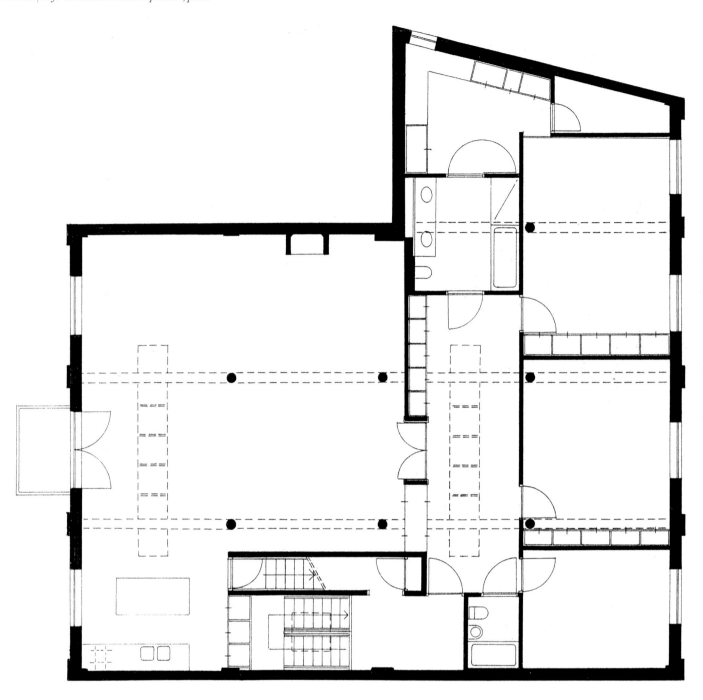

ACKNOWLEDGEMENTS

Like so many other books, *Lofts of Amsterdam* has been a long-term project. We would therefore like first of all to thank our sponsor, Isis Beheer B.V. Tilburg, because they have continued to support us fully to the very end.

Particular thanks go to all the people who have helped us looking for addresses of lofts or put us in contact with loft-dwellers. In this respect, special thanks to Frits de Kousemaeker, Grace Locations, the architects Roberto Meyer, Jaap Dijckman, Rudy Uytenhaak, George Witteveen and Pim Köther, the interior designer Wim De Vos and the Hemo Misker location agency.

We would also like to thank the whole *Lofts of Amsterdam* team: the photographers Guy Obijn, Diederik van der Mieden and Jo Jetten, the editors Yvonne Cox and Bert Verbeke, the designer Mark Leytens and the translator Gregory Ball.

RUDY STEVENS & PHILIPPE DE BAECK
Antwerp, October 2000

CREDITLINE

Frontcover left: Jo Jetten; frontcover right: Jo Jetten; backcover: Guy Obijn; backcover flap: Guy Obijn

BOOKWORK: p 2-3: Jo Jetten; p 4: Jo Jetten; pp 6-7: Jo Jetten; p10: Jo Jetten; pp 16-17: Living...and working: Jo Jetten; pp 18-21: The art of omission: Guy Obijn; pp 22-25: Crack the safe: Guy Obijn; pp 26-33: Art at home: Jo Jetten; pp 34-35: Rural scenes: Jo Jetten; pp 36-39: Life is a process of growth: Diederik van der Mieden; pp 40-43: Self devised and homemade: Guy Obijn; pp 44-47: From Picasso to Wolkers: Jo Jetten; pp 48-49: Open lofts: Jo Jetten; pp 50-53: From stable to mega-loft: Diederik van der Mieden; pp 54-57: Living in boxes: Diederik van der Mieden; pp 58-63: Electric Blue: Diederik van der Mieden; pp 64-69: Materials speak for themselves: Guy Obijn; pp 70-75: View of the city: Jo Jetten; pp 76-79: School of original design: Guy Obijn; pp 80-83: Lightfactory: Guy Obijn; pp 84-85: Commercial premises: Guy Obijn; pp 86-89: Where even the client is one of the family: Jo Jetten; pp 90-91: Design in shipping containers: Guy Obijn; pp 92-95: An office as quiet as a church: Guy Obijn en Jeroen Musch; pp 96-101: Warehouse 'Pakhuis Amsterdam': Diederik van der Mieden; pp 102-103: Collectors: Diederik van der Mieden; pp 104-107: Where history is alive: Jo Jetten; pp 108-113: A Venetian palazzo: Guy Obijn; pp 114-117: In a colonial atmosphere: Guy Obijn; pp 118-121: Sugar-sweet romanticism: Diederik van der Mieden; pp 122-125: Antique modernism: Diederik van der Mieden; pp 126-129: Narda's ark: Diederik van der Mieden; pp 130-133: A marvellous world in an old bank building: Guy Obijn; pp 134-137: The good Samaritan: Jo Jetten; pp 138-139: Churches: Guy Obijn; pp 140-145: Shelter in a church: Guy Obijn; pp 146-149: 'Imps & Elfs' over the font: Guy Obijn; pp 150-153: Plain luxury: Guy Obijn; pp 154-157: A lamp is the prayer, the law a light: Guy Obijn; pp 158-163: A heavenly home: Guy Obijn; pp 164-165: H2O: Mirande Phernampucq; pp 166-169: Emma's island: Jo Jetten; pp 170-171: On the waterside of the world: Diederik van der Mieden; pp 172-175: Welcome on board: Diederik van der Mieden; pp 176-179: Boatbuilder becomes loft-builder: Jo Jetten; pp 180-181: From Jugendstil to minimalism: Jo Jetten; pp 182-185: Gietershof: Jo Jetten; pp 186-189: A ray of sunshine in the house: Diederik van der Mieden; pp 190-193: That orange feeling: Jo Jetten; pp 194-199: Loft with allure: Guy Obijn; pp 200-203: One-arm bandits: Jo Jetten; pp 204-207: 't Blaeuwe Huys: Jo Jetten; pp 208-209: Coloured grey: Guy Obijn; pp 210-213: Colour galore: Diederik van der Mieden and Guy Obijn; pp 214-219: Africa blues: Guy Obijn; pp 220-223: Green Oasis in the city centre: Jo Jetten; pp 224-227: Surprise Corners, study rooms: Diederik van der Mieden; pp 228-231: How perception can make something small into something grand: Diederik van der Mieden; p 246: Jo Jetten.